Original title:
Tales of the Tall Trees

Copyright © 2025 Creative Arts Management OÜ
All rights reserved.

Author: Alexander Thornton
ISBN HARDBACK: 978-1-80567-404-7
ISBN PAPERBACK: 978-1-80567-703-1

Beneath the Boundless Timber

In the forest, squirrels dance,
Chasing shadows, taking a chance.
A bear in slippers, oh what a sight,
Stumbling over roots in morning light.

Owls gossip loudly, perched so high,
While raccoons plot, oh my, oh my!
Beneath branches, a party unfolds,
With laughter and mischief, stories are told.

Narratives in Nature's Embrace

A chipmunk wearing a tiny hat,
Danced on a log, how about that!
Birds form a band, singing their tune,
While deer join in like a birthday balloon.

Trees whisper secrets in the breeze,
As bees buzz around with utmost ease.
Each leaf a page, a giggle contained,
Nature's memoirs, humor unrestrained.

The Wisdom of Wooded Kings

Beneath the boughs of ancient kings,
A raccoon's crown and a squirrel's bling.
They debate the best nut pie to bake,
In a banquet of berries, for fun's sake!

Wise old owls share chuckles at night,
While fireflies perform in dazzling light.
Candid chatter fills the cool dark,
Nature's comedy, a vibrant spark.

The Lullabies of Leaves

A leaf fell down just to take a dive,
Landed on a snail, and said, "Let's jive!"
Crickets played maracas, with great flair,
While frogs leapt up, diving with flair.

Each whispering breeze shares humorous tales,
Of hedgehogs dressed up in grand details.
The moonlight chuckles, the sunbeam winks,
In this lively world, everyone thinks.

The Still Voice of the Silvers

In a grove where whispers dance,
A squirrel plans his great romance.
With acorns piled high to impress,
For nuts, he'll wear a tiny dress.

The birch tree chuckles, leaves a-flutter,
"Who knew a critter could be a nutter?"
While owls roll eyes in wise surprise,
Just laugh along with those bright skies!

Seasoned Stories of Stillness

A hedgehog says, "I've tales to share,"
Of secret paths and fragrant air.
"I once tripped over a turtle slow,
Turtledom's finest, ten years in tow!"

The pine trees nod with gentle grace,
Their needles tickle, a funny space.
"Next time, leave the racing to the hares,
And trade your speed for nature's wares!"

Rhapsody in the Rustling Foliage

A funky frog sings in the reeds,
"I hop, I croak, I plant some seeds!"
With swing and sway in leafy choir,
He strums a twig—what a wild flyer!

"Watch out, dear friend, for flying ants,
They're dressed in suits, but cannot dance."
The willows giggle, swaying low,
As ants parade, all set to show!

Voyage Through Verdant Towers

The tall trees tower, roots entwined,
Their branches twist in tales enshrined.
A parrot jokes, "What's up, my dude?
A worm just asked for 'good' food!"

"A feast of leaves, a buffet grand,
Join in the fun, make leafy bands!"
The chitter-chatter fills the wood,
With laughter blooming where life's good!

Canopy Coils

In the treetops, squirrels bicker,
Climbing high, they play and snicker.
One lost a nut, it fell with a plop,
Now he's searching, can't seem to stop.

A bird on a branch sings a tune,
While a raccoon dances, quite a cartoon.
The leaves giggle as breezes blow,
Rustling secrets only they know.

Secrets of the Silent Sentinels

Old trunks whisper, wise and grand,
Telling tales of a squirrel band.
They plan a fiesta, snacks to share,
With acorns and berries; without a care.

A rabbit hops by, wearing a hat,
"Is this the party? Tell me, where's that?"
The trees chuckle at the mix-up so bright,
While fireflies prepare to light up the night.

From the Roots to the Sky

Down below, worms dance in a line,
Cheering the ants, oh, what a time!
Up above, a raccoon swings about,
While a nervous crow tries not to shout.

Branches sway like silly straws,
Rooting for critters without a pause.
The sun pokes through, a spotlight indeed,
For nature's goofballs to take the lead.

Ballads of the Wind-Worn Wood

The wind strums branches, a funny tune,
While critters gather, under the moon.
"Let's sing a song about our fun lives,
With snorts and giggles, as nature thrives!"

The owls hoot, trying to keep pace,
Mischievous squirrels race in a chase.
All around, the forest joins in,
A merry ballet, let the laughter begin!

Dreaming Under the Canopy

When the squirrels start to chatter,
I giggle at their endless rattle.
They plot their acorn heist with flair,
While I drift in my comfy chair.

Frogs croak jokes, it's quite the show,
With tangled vines, they steal the glow.
The sun peeks through, a wink or two,
As leaves gossip about the dew.

Each branch a giant swing of wit,
Where nature's laughter seems to fit.
Mice host dances under the moon,
Even ants play a merry tune.

Vistas of the Vertical Realm

Look up high, what a wild sight,
Frogs in tuxedos, what a fright!
They hop and skip with such great glee,
While birds critique with cup of tea.

A raccoon dons a cap and gown,
Outsmarting shadows of the town.
As branches sway with comedy,
I laugh along with every tree.

And owls, wise but a little crude,
Tell tales that leave us all in mood.
With every twist, the branches bend,
Nature's jest that won't yet end.

The Chronicles of Crests and Canopies

In the heart of woods, it's playtime show,
Squirrels skate in a nutty glow.
Each branch a stage for their bright skit,
While chipmunks rush, they never sit.

A lizard quips, then strikes a pose,
As shadows samba, nobody knows.
The breeze carries chuckles and spins,
Welcome to the circus where laughter wins.

Eagles glide, with a wink they dive,
Fetching the humor, they feel so alive.
Leaves tickle the birds in flight,
In this green world, all's pure delight.

Footfalls in the Forest

With every step, the forest giggles,
Each twig a voice, each leaf a wriggle.
The path is dotted with whimsical sights,
As mushrooms dance with playful lights.

Beneath the boughs, the ground does chuckle,
While rabbits tease with their quick shuffle.
Badgers tell tales with a sly grin,
In this stitched-up mat of green and sin.

Crickets chirp with wisecracks bold,
As whispers of greenery continue to fold.
The trees, they tickle with every breeze,
Nature's humor, such joy to seize.

Whispers of the Ancient Canopy

In the branches where squirrels play,
One tells a joke to chase clouds away.
Leaves rustle, giggles in the breeze,
Even the owls chuckle with ease.

A raccoon dons a hat of twigs,
Says he's off to dance with the big pigs.
Beneath a moon, they spin and cheer,
While trees sway gently, lending an ear.

Secrets Beneath the Giants

A turtle whispers tales of race,
With snails claiming it's all in good pace.
Under the roots, a mouse dons a crown,
Shouting, "I'm king in this underground town!"

Ants line up for a grand parade,
Marching to tunes that the earth has played.
Every bug jives, a hilarious sight,
Even the beetles rolled over in delight.

Shadows Dance in Leafy Heights

Frogs leap higher than they ever should,
In search of snacks, they're up to no good.
The shadows laugh at their clumsy falls,
As critters gather to witness it all.

A parrot squawks, "Let's have a ball!"
He ropes in rabbits, they answer the call.
With twirls and hops, they create a scene,
In the leafy heights, merry and keen.

Echoes of the Forest's Spine

Beneath the boughs, a party unfolds,
With critters and giggles, legends retold.
Rabbits wear shoes made of grass and mud,
While chipmunks giggle, "Let's dance in the crud!"

The wind joins in with a playful tune,
Whispers of laughter beneath the moon.
Each creature sways in delightful sync,
Mischief and joy in every blink.

The Spirit of the Tall Ones

In the woods, the tall folks dance,
Their leafy hats in a merry prance.
They tickle the clouds with roots of glee,
Whispering secrets to you and me.

A squirrel laughs at a joke so grand,
While rabbits join in, hand in hand.
Branches sway with a giggle and twist,
Who knew trees had such a twisty list?

Woodpeckers tap a jolly beat,
Doing the cha-cha with tiny feet.
Beverages flow from a flowing stream,
The forest holds its wildest dream!

So next time you stroll where the tall ones sway,
Listen closely, they'll brighten your day!
With laughter echoing through leafy halls,
The spirit of fun in nature calls.

Beneath the Skyward Branches

Beneath the branches, shadows play,
A raccoon wears a hat made of hay.
The owls hoot jokes from high above,
Squirrels crack nuts with all their love.

In twilight's glow, the fireflies blink,
While frogs come out for a fashion wink.
Each leaf flutters with tales of cheer,
As crickets chirp, 'The party's here!'

Mice in tuxedos dance a fine jig,
While a wise old fox hums a short gig.
Twisting and twirling, they spin around,
Joy in the heart of this vibrant ground.

So when shadows stretch and night takes flight,
Join the revels till morning light!
For under the trees where laughter rings,
You'll find the joy that nature brings.

Refuge of the Narrow Leaves

In a nook where narrow leaves collide,
A playful pixie takes a ride.
On a leaf boat, he sails with flair,
Inviting all to join the dare!

The ants parade in a funky line,
Dressed in colors, looking so fine.
Each tiny foot taps out a beat,
Creating rhythms that can't be beat!

A turtle joins, with a smile so wide,
Says, 'Slow and steady, let's enjoy the ride!'
While spiders weave a disco ball,
Shining bright in the forest hall.

So seek this refuge where laughter thrives,
In the company of nature, joy arrives!
When narrow leaves flutter and spin,
The heart of the woodland lets the fun begin!

The Singing of the Saplings

Saplings sway in harmony,
Each one hums a note of glee.
With wind as their musical guide,
They laugh, they play, they dance, they glide.

A chipmunk taps a tiny drum,
While bright butterflies beat the strum.
Together they brew a lively tune,
Under the bright and smiling moon.

The chorus rings through every space,
Join in the song, find your pace!
For nature's music is never far,
Just listen close beneath the stars.

So sway with the saplings, dance along,
Let yourself join this merry throng!
In each rustling leaf, a giggle waits,
Come out and play, open those gates!

Lullabies from the Canopied Heights

In the treetops, squirrels tease,
Chasing each other with such ease.
A raccoon sings, it's quite absurd,
While a wise owl hoots, unheard.

Branches sway with laughter loud,
Frogs wear crowns, feeling proud.
A squirrel juggles acorns with flair,
As chipmunks dance without a care.

The breeze carries tales of cheer,
Of mischief in every ear.
Bouncing leaves join in the fun,
As sunlight plays, the day is won.

So rest your head, drift and dream,
Of forest antics and giggling streams.
For up above, the laughter's clear,
In the heights where joy draws near.

The Gnarled Chronicles of Old

Beneath the branches, stories stir,
With mushrooms chatting as they purr.
Old gnarled trunks, with tales to tell,
Of cheeky knots and laughs that swell.

A squirrel claims a throne of leaves,
While a badger schemes and weaves.
Whispers float on the breeze so bright,
As trees conspire to delight the night.

Acorns ring like tiny bells,
As woodpeckers drum their spells.
Each nook and cranny holds a grin,
Where laughter echoes, and fun begins.

In the twilight, shadows play,
Beneath the stars, they shout hooray!
For every driftwood tale is bold,
In the gnarled world of wonders told.

Fables Woven in Green Gables

In green gables, rabbits hop,
Wearing hats and spinning tops.
A hedgehog plays the violin,
While crickets dance and twirl within.

The grass whispers secrets of delight,
As butterflies flutter soft and light.
Every turn brings giggles anew,
With a frog conducting the band of dew.

Trees play hide and seek at dusk,
While fireflies flash, it's quite a must!
Squirrels in costume make a scene,
In this whimsical, vibrant green.

Under moonlight, the fables gleam,
Full of mischief, twist, and dream.
Join in the laughter, let it flow,
For green gables hold delight in tow.

Legends Carved in Nature's Embrace

In the embrace of leaves, they prance,
Creatures join in a merry dance.
A bear holds court with a fishy tale,
While rabbits giggle, bright and pale.

Legends told of undergrowth's cheer,
Where gnomes play cards, never fear!
A fox in boots struts with grace,
As tales unfold in this lively space.

Trees lean in, their bark a grin,
As secrets spin and joys begin.
A chorus of laughter fills the air,
In legends carved, beyond compare.

So gather round, let stories race,
In nature's arms, we find our place.
With every twist, a chuckle grows,
In this embrace where silliness flows.

Chronicles of the Forest's Heart

In the woods where critters prance,
Squirrels hold a dance-off chance.
Raccoons juggle shiny things,
While rabbits gossip about their rings.

The owl hoots a comedy show,
Beneath the stars that brightly glow.
Each tree leans in, ears perked wide,
As laughter dances in the countryside.

Frogs in tuxedos hop with flair,
To serenade the evening air.
With wise old trees in hearty cheer,
Each chuckle echoes far and near.

Breezes carry giggles past,
As nature's jokes are unsurpassed.
The forest bursts, a joyful spree,
Where humor grows on every tree.

Under the Grand Arches

Under arches grand and wide,
The squirrels slide like they're on a ride.
A woodpecker plays a drumbeat loud,
As the trees jiggle, oh so proud.

With branches swinging, vines that twist,
A mist of laughter can't be missed.
The porcupines tell jokes so sharp,
That even the skunks can't help but harp.

Beneath the leaves, a picnic scene,
Ants dressed up in shiny sheen.
Carrying crumbs, all in a row,
Their tiny feet tap to the show.

The sun peeks down, a joker bright,
Paints the forest in pure delight.
Nature chuckles, a funny spree,
Beneath the arches, wild and free.

Stories of the Verdant Watchers

The watchful trees with faces so wide,
Crack jokes while the forest animals hide.
A fox rolls back with laughter's cheer,
As leaves shake gently, bringing near.

The bushes brew tales, twisted and fun,
Of a turtle that raced a quick little bun.
Later a snail, with swagger and style,
Claimed he'd win, but stayed for a while.

A bear in a hat, telling tall tales,
While turtles gossip in winding trails.
With raccoon snickers and chittering blue,
Each story unfolds like morning dew.

At dusk, as shadows begin to dash,
The forest whispers in a playful splash.
Verdant watchers laugh with glee,
As moonlight plays, wild and free.

The Sylvan Symphony

In the symphony where the wild things play,
The trees hum soft, as if to say,
"Grab your friends, it's jam time here,
Join the chorus, spread the cheer!"

A squirrel strums on a tiny lute,
While chipmunks tap their chubby foot.
The owls blink with rhythm divine,
As crickets croon a tune so fine.

The winds join in with a swirling sound,
Whispers flutter as joy abounds.
With notes that flutter like leaves in fall,
Each harmony rises, uniting all.

At twilight's hush, the concert grows bright,
Stars twirl in the sky, a shimmering sight.
Nature's laughter and melody rare,
The sylvan symphony fills the air.

Wisdom in the Rings of Time

In the shade where squirrels dance,
The wise old tree gives every chance.
With a creak and a groan, he shares a joke,
While the birds laugh hard 'til they almost choke.

Each knot a story, each branch a plot,
"Once I met a leaf that couldn't trot!"
Twisting roots that tickle the ground,
Such wisdom here is quite profound!

Rings that number with such glee,
Count the years, but who's to see?
A raccoon whispers in the breeze,
"Trees don't weed; they just say, 'Please!'"

Nuts and seeds, a tree's delight,
Tales of acorns take their flight.
Bounce a fruit, watch it fall,
The wisdom's there for one and all!

The Heartbeat of the Grove

The trees all sway to a quirky beat,
With roots that tap and branches that greet.
A woodpecker drums a hearty tune,
While the leaves shimmy under the moon.

In the grove, there's laughter galore,
As critters dance on the forest floor.
"Join the fun!" the trunks all shout,
"Life's a party, no doubt!"

A glittering breeze comes sailing through,
With each rustle, a joke's slipped anew.
"Why did the twig break?" they jest with glee,
"Because it couldn't handle the tree-ology!"

Clouds drift by in a silly way,
Casting shadows that jig and sway.
A chipmunk shimmies, the oak claps hands,
In this grove, humor forever stands!

Soliloquies from the Towering Boughs

Up high where the view looks bright,
Tall stories spill in the fading light.
"Who needs a crown when you've got this height?"
Claims the tree with a laugh and delight.

The branches gossip of passing birds,
In wacky whispers, with silly words.
"Did you hear that squirrel tried to fly?
He landed on a pineapple pie!"

Beneath the boughs a critter crew,
Swapping tales amid the morning dew.
"I fell asleep with a wink and a nod,
Awoke to find I'd been used as a rod!"

So listen close to their woody chime,
Each branch holds secrets that tickle with rhyme.
Nature's jesters, they sway and sway,
Bringing laughter to the light of day!

Celestial Vistas Through Ferny Lenses

With ferns that dance like they're on toast,
The tall trees sway, they love to boast.
"Look at me, I'm reaching for stars!
I even waved at passing cars!"

A green canopy with giggles so loud,
Whispers tales to the wandering crowd.
"Did you see the owl in pajamas last night?
He missed his flight and just took a bite!"

The moon peeks through with a wink that gleams,
Illuminating the woodland's dreams.
Raccoons giggle at a star's silly face,
"In the dark, even stars need a place!"

Through ferny lenses, life's a spree,
Every glance reveals more to see.
Up high, the laughter rings crystal clear,
Nature's joy — let's all draw near!

Guardians of the Woodland Sky

In a realm where the squirrels play,
Chasing shadows throughout the day.
A wise old owl starts to hoot,
While rabbits dance in funky boots.

The trees wear hats of leafy green,
Where critters gather for the scene.
The raccoons tell their finest jokes,
As laughter echoes, poking folks.

Mice practice acrobatic flips,
While hedgehogs wear their tinyhips.
The ants debate who's truly boss,
Amidst the fun, they handle loss.

So if you wander through this maze,
Join in the woodland's crazy ways.
With giggles loud and spirits free,
Life's a laugh in this grand spree.

The Veil of Verdant Legends

Among the ferns so lush and grand,
A gnome with dreams cooked up a plan.
To brew a potion made of dew,
And teach the trees a dance or two.

The fairies twirl with sparkling lights,
Flapping wings and joyous flights.
"Who needs gravity?" they cheer,
As they flip and spin without a fear.

The badger writes a comic strip,
While foxes take the stage and skip.
The bushes chuckle, roots do sway,
In this wood, the fun won't fray.

So raise a cup of acorn tea,
To woodland friends and jubilee.
In every nook, a happy tune,
Beneath the sun and goofy moon.

Sagas of the Timbered Realm

In a kingdom high with branches wide,
A turtle rides a bouncy tide.
With hats of moss and shoes of bark,
They host a party in the dark.

An owl brings cupcakes, oh so sweet,
While chipmunks compete for the best seat.
Grinning, they dance around the fire,
While the stars watch with pure desire.

The wise old tree starts to recite,
The most ridiculous tales of fright.
As creatures laugh, spitting out cheese,
Not a scare, just giggles in the breeze.

So if you hear a raucous cheer,
Know that frolics bring joy near.
In timbered realms of fun and cheer,
Every creature holds laughter dear.

Where the Sky Meets the Bark

Where the clouds wear their fluffy crowns,
The woodland breaks into giggly towns.
A squirrel juggles acorns, quite a show,
While below, the flowers buzz and glow.

A hedgehog prances on tightropes fine,
With a confident swish and a glimmering shine.
The bees gossip of blossoms new,
As butterflies join in with a woohoo.

The trees giggle with rustling leaves,
Telling tales of their great thieves.
Who took the last sunbeam, who's to blame?
In this world, every laugh's a game.

So leap between roots, and laugh with glee,
Join nature's chorus in sweet decree.
For where the sky meets age-old bark,
Lies a kingdom bright, and always stark.

Enchanted Heights

In a forest where squirrels wear hats,
The rabbits debate over top-hat stats.
Branches swing low with giggle and cheer,
While frogs in tuxedos croon songs we hear.

High above, a sloth tried to show,
His dance moves but moved way too slow.
The owl took a nap on a branch of foam,
While the raccoons planned a midnight roam.

The acorns drop like marbles from trees,
Landing on pillows of leaves with ease.
And in this place of silliness tall,
Even the shadows break into a sprawl.

When a woodpecker sings in a quirky way,
All the critters gather; it's their fun day.
With laughter that echoes, they sing and swing,
In the enchanted heights where the cuckoo can sing.

Whispering Woods, Legends Woven in Starlit Branches.

In a glade where the fireflies flash,
The pixies get ready for a silly bash.
With cupcakes made of moss and dew,
A cake-walk competition is long overdue.

Beetles march in their shiny parade,
While slugs slide in, unplanned and displayed.
A raccoon juggles with berries and twigs,
His audience roars—these woodland big wigs!

Under starlit branches, they weave their lore,
Of owls who slipped and rolled on the floor.
They laugh as the night sky gives them a show,
In the whispering woods where the fun takes a flow.

As the moon winks down, they dance with might,
Each leaf a participant in their delight.
With stories of whimsy, they cozy and cheer,
In this lively land where all are most dear.

Whispers of the Canopy

In the canopy high, a giggle takes flight,
As squirrels play tag in the warm sunlight.
A wise old tree with a face full of bark,
Tells jokes to the leaves, and they giggle back, hark!

The parrot dressed up in a vibrant crayon,
Plays tricks on the owls who just yawn and yawn.
But the chameleon slips, and what a wild sight,
He turns polka-dots in mid-air, quite the fright!

With whispers of mischief that sway in the breeze,
The shadows come out to dance with such ease.
And as twilight falls, the canopy glows,
With laughter and stories that nobody knows.

As acorns rain down like tiny balloons,
The creatures all gather and sing silly tunes.
In a world that is leafy, lively, and spry,
The whispers of joy make the evening fly by.

Giants in the Green

Giants in the green with their roots held tight,
They chuckle at clouds with all their might.
The breeze comes to play, tickling their leaves,
While the chipmunks scurry and weave through the eaves.

With laughter that rolls through bark and through soil,
They whisper of days when the sun made them toil.
The mushrooms attend their annual show,
Where each fungi struts, putting on quite the glow!

As the twilight creeps in, the stars take their seats,
The shadows around dance on wiggly feet.
And the deer tell tall tales to the boughs up above,
Of who's the best dancer in the forest of love.

So join in the fun and get lost in the scene,
With giants and critters who twirl in between.
For in every whisper, so much joy is found,
In the green of the woods, with laughter all 'round.

The Symphony of Sage Branches

In the forest where squirrels plot,
They dance on branches, a merry lot.
With acorn hats and twigs for toys,
They sing out loud with tiny joys.

The wind joins in, a playful friend,
As leaves start swirling, twists and bends.
A melody of rustle, snap,
Nature's concert, no time for a nap.

The wise old owl joins the chorus,
Blasting notes that astound us.
With a hoot, he claims his place,
In this raucous, leaf-laden space.

A tree who juggles stones with flair,
Befriends a raccoon with unkempt hair.
They laugh as they tumble in cheer,
Creating a symphony, never austere.

Murmurs of the Stalwart Stems

Stalwart stems stand tall and proud,
With whispers shared amongst the crowd.
They gossip 'bout the critters' plays,
Finding humor in their clumsy ways.

A bumblebee in a dandy suit,
Buzzes about, sharp as a flute.
He trips on petals, oh what a sight,
Adventures abound from morning to night.

The trunks sway gently, tales they weave,
Of mischief and pranks that none would believe.
Like the ant who wore an oversized shoe,
He parades around, thinking it's cool.

Each crack in the bark tells a joke,
Of wayward winds and the trees they stoke.
Together they giggle, in unison cheer,
In this serene place, full of good cheer.

Echoing Dreams in the Boughs

Dreams echo through the branches wide,
As giggles of squirrels cannot hide.
A dream of nuts, a glorious gain,
In leafy halls, they dance and feign.

A note from a bird, cheerful and bright,
Whispers of pies baked in the night.
The branches sway, a waltz they spin,
As branches nudge, let the fun begin!

With twinkling stars peeking below,
The nightly plays put on quite a show.
Owls chuckle low, 'What a sight to see!'
As raccoons bicker over a berry spree.

Through all the jest, these dreams take flight,
In the boughs, laughter echoes, pure delight.
Together they revel, in joyous beams,
As the woods embrace their silly dreams.

Unraveled Myths Among the Leaves

Amidst the leaves, stories unfold,
Of playful gnomes and secrets told.
A tiny sprout with a grand old dream,
Relished in laughter, bursting at the seam.

With each gust of wind, a tale to share,
Of nutty squirrels who dare and dare.
A clever fox with a jester's knack,
Who ne'er wore a single shade of black.

The leaves, they rustle, an uproarious jest,
As critters gather, they're at their best.
With acorns tossed and merry delight,
The stories bloom in the soft moonlight.

From whispers deep, to hearty guffaws,
Each creature's aim, to spark applause.
In the antics of nature, joy is rife,
As the trees chuckle at this circus of life.

Sagas of the Whispering Woods

In the woods where shadows play,
Squirrels dance and chirp all day.
Barking trees with hats askew,
Laughing leaves have jokes for you.

Birds in coats of bright satin,
Tell tall tales of Mr. Bat-in.
A wise old owl spins yarns quite bold,
While hedgehogs laugh, "Man, we're told!"

Rabbits gossip, foxes grin,
Mysteries linger like a din.
As branches sway in fits of glee,
The woods chuckle, "Come join me!"

In this land of merry lore,
Every creature's a "forest whore."
We trip on roots with giddy cries,
Making friends with every sigh.

The Heartbeat of the Forest

Beneath the stars, all critters hum,
Dance to the rhythm of the drum.
Bears in pajamas, grinning wide,
March to the beat, with a playful stride.

Raccoons in top hats, sipping tea,
Chat about who's the best on a spree.
Pointy eared gossipers take flight,
Stealing the show in the moonlight.

Twinkling fireflies flash a grin,
"Did you hear how the turtle wins?"
Grass blades giggle with each breeze,
Even the mushrooms sway with ease.

As laughter echoes through each nook,
Every cranny is our storybook.
Join the party, don't be shy,
In the heart where the forests sigh.

Conversations with the Old Ones

The ancient oaks have tales to share,
With mossy beards and gnarled hair.
They tell of squirrels with grand designs,
Plotting parties, dodging fines.

"Once I saw a frog in socks,"
Said one old stump, "While shouting 'knocks!'
He jumped so high, I lost my bark,
And now I'm just a stump in the park."

Rabbits chimed, "Oh please, that's rich!"
While hedgehogs snickered, "What a glitch!"
With every tale, the laughter flows,
Old trees giggle, their spirits glow.

So gather 'round when day is done,
Join in the laughter, it's all in fun.
The forest thrives on silly screams,
Where ancient whispers meet wild dreams.

Majestic Heights

Up in the branches, high and spry,
Eagles plot how to wave goodbye.
"Look at me!" boasts the tallest pine,
"King of the woods, on a slippery line!"

Parrots squawk, "You think you're grand?
We're the jesters in this land!"
Flying high with feathers spread,
Tickling the clouds, they dance like Fred.

"Why did the crow cross the road?"
"Oh look, there's a turtle with a load!"
Whispers echo with jokes untold,
The tall trees laugh as the tales unfold.

With each sway in the gentle breeze,
They engage in a playful tease.
So climb with courage, just don't fall,
In the heights, nature's a comedy hall.

Silent Stories

In the quiet glades where secrets hide,
The frogs in silence take great pride.
Telling stories without a sound,
As hidden fairies dance around.

The mushrooms giggle, keeping watch,
On midnight calls from the garden's botch.
With whispers soft as autumn's sighs,
Beneath the stars, mischief flies.

The moonlight glimmers on old trunks,
As crickets chirp their little funks.
"Did you hear?" one willow bemoans,
"I once dated a pine, but he moans!"

In shadows deep, the night becomes,
A canvas painted with silly drums.
Here stories rest without a sound,
Yet in their silence, laughter's found.

The Soul of the Oak

In the shade of the old oak's grin,
Squirrels tell secrets of where they've been.
With acorns dancing in their paws,
They debate the best nutty flaws.

The oak chuckles, its branches sway,
"You won't catch me in a nutty play!"
As birds chirp gossip from high above,
Creating a ruckus, a tree-folk love.

Rabbits hop by with a twitching nose,
"Did you hear the news? The moss garden grows!"
The oak just sighs, rolling its bark,
"Those rumors spread faster than a lark!"

In the heart of this leafy space,
Everyone's welcome, no need for a race.
They'll laugh and jest until sundown,
In the oak's shade, no need for a crown.

Fables from the Forest Floor

Down on the forest floor, what a sight!
Frogs are hosting a dance party tonight.
With lily pad stages and tadpole bands,
They croak out tunes with a splash from their hands.

A raccoon, dressed up, spins round the log,
Proclaiming loudly, "I'm the best in the fog!"
The snails move slowly, but have a style,
Wearing little hats, they glisten and smile.

Beneath the tall ferns, a tiny farce,
A beetle trips over a blushing grass.
With a roll and a tumble, it joins the fun,
The laughter erupts under the setting sun.

In this woodland jest, everyone's a star,
From the ladybugs to the squirrels afar.
No need for a stage or a big costume,
Just join in the fun, let your joy bloom!

Enchanted in the Embrace

In a hollow tree, the owls convene,
To share their tales of the night unseen.
With big wide eyes and feathers all fluffed,
They giggle at shadows, and act rather tough.

Whispers of spells float on the breeze,
While busy ants march with utmost ease.
"Why don't we conjure some snacks for this crew?"
Said the wise old owl, with a wink and a coo.

But spells often flop, an enchanting mess,
Turning acorns to pies, what a silly guess!
The forest bursts forth with munching delight,
"Who knew a spell could taste just right?"

So they feast and they laugh, till the morning arrives,
Embracing the joy in their crazy lives.
Under the branches where fun brightly plays,
The forest remembers its magical days.

Tales of the Verdant Guardians

Amidst the greenery, the guardians chat,
A turtle brags, "I'll outrun that cat!"
A wise old owl hoots, "You may have a shell,
But move like molasses, you're slow as a bell!"

The hedgehog giggles, rolling in glee,
Said, "I'm quite prickly, come challenge me!"
With thorns standing tall, it stands to defend,
"I bet you all wish you could call me friend!"

They swap silly stories of the forest quest,
A raccoon in pajamas, always dressed best.
The laughter echoes through the towering maze,
Where each guardian's antics find splendid praise.

So under the canopy, what a crew!
The forest's green laughter, both silly and true.
With friendship and fun, they thrive and they play,
In their verdant domain, come night or come day!

Serenades of the Sylvan Splendor

In a forest quite grand, where the squirrels race,
A hedgehog wore goggles, a curious face.
The trees chuckled softly with every high tail,
As the owls joined the laughter, revealing their pale.

Amidst all the chuckles, a deer tried to dance,
With two left feet, it took quite the chance.
The branches swayed gently, in rhythm and glee,
While the flowers all giggled, oh, what a spree!

A raccoon played piano, oh, what a sight,
His tiny paws slipping, but his tunes took flight.
With a pause and a grin, he'd turn to the crowd,
And the woodpeckers hooted, so proud and so loud.

Thus in this green haven, where nonsense is key,
Nature holds revels, so wild and so free.
For in every tall trunk and each rustling leaf,
Lies a spirit of laughter, beyond all belief.

Forgotten Echoes on Windy Paths

On pathways well-worn, where the breezes play,
A crow wore a hat, claiming it was his day.
He cawed with great flair, a real show-off chap,
While the turtles just laughed, caught up in the flap.

"Good sir!" said the rabbit, in a top hat quite neat,
"Your style is quite daring—now strut on your feet!"
But the crow, ever proud, just rustled his wing,
And the frogs joined the chorus, belting their swing.

As shadows grew long, the sunset's soft beam,
A wise old fox whispered, "Let's join in this dream."
With a twist and a turn, they all hopped along,
While the chirpy crickets played a funky old song.

Forgotten were worries beneath the tall trees,
As time ticked away, lost in giggles and ease.
With echoes of joy in the wind as they passed,
On these winding paths, happiness was cast.

Reveries in Rooted Realms

In realms where roots tangle and branches entwine,
A chipmunk with shades felt truly divine.
He sipped on a nut, with a wink and a grin,
Said, "Life's just a party—let the fun begin!"

An ant wore a crown, quite proud of his reign,
While the beetles performed in their jazzy domain.
With rhythms so lively, a dance they all choreographed,
And even the snails gave a cheerful little laugh.

The mushrooms all giggled, in colors so bright,
While dancing in circles, what a hilarious sight!
With laughter and joy weaving through every bough,
It was clear that this realm knew exactly how.

So here in the roots, where the mischief is sown,
Life is a comedy—better shared than alone!
Each creature a player in this woodland cheer,
With every delight echoing loud and clear.

The Chronicle of the Arboreal Realm

In the deep of the woods where the tall trunks arise,
A squirrel told stories that sparked laughing eyes.
He juggled his acorns, a daring display,
While the rabbits all cheered, hip-hip-hooray!

A wise old owl hooted, "Let's make this a jest!"
With feathers all fluffed, he put humor to test.
But every wise word got tangled in fun,
As the badger joined in, proclaiming he'd run!

And the bumblebees buzzed, with comical flair,
As they danced in the air, playing tag with a hare.
With nature as witness, their antics astound,
In this arboreal place, laughter's always found.

So cherish the whispers from trees standing tall,
For in every chuckle, you'll find joy for all.
In this chronicled life, where humor has flown,
The heart of the forest feels wondrously known.

The Mind of the Wooded Titans

In the forest, whispers play,
Where squirrels debate and sway.
Acorns have a secret club,
Laughing over every grub.

The owls hoot their wise old tune,
Claiming stars will dance by noon.
Rabbits race with silly cheer,
While shadows chuckle, never fear.

A fox with a monocle and hat,
Analyzes a sleeping cat.
Laughter echoes through the green,
As mischief thrives, unnoticed, unseen.

Tall titans with their leafy crowns,
Giggle softly, wearing frowns.
For who can fathom their delight,
In games of hide and seek by night?

Silhouettes of Time Under Canopies

Underneath the leafy quilt,
Time prances, with no guilt.
Chipmunks hold a jolly feast,
Beneath their bark-skinned priest.

Shadows strut in silly dance,
While squirrels jump at every chance.
Each rustle brings a chuckling grin,
As branches shake with fits within.

Old trunks tell tales of years gone by,
In hushed tones and a lopsided sigh.
They gossip low, in breezy tones,
About the creatures, their silly bones.

Through the glade, the sunbeams flirt,
With mossy toes and wild shirt.
Perhaps they'll tease the clumsy frog,
Who trips on roots, back into the bog.

Whimsy Beneath the Rustic Arches

Beneath the boughs, a party brews,
With buzzing bees and happy snooze.
Mice don tiny, festive hats,
As hedgehogs spin like acrobats.

Bark boats float on puddle streams,
Filled with laughter, food, and dreams.
Fireflies twinkle like fairy lights,
While frogs croak jokes in frothy sights.

Breezy whispers hold the tune,
As elders sway beneath the moon.
Wily raccoons, with cheeky grins,
Collect the spoils of playful sins.

Time skips lightly on dampened grass,
In a world where giggles pass.
Under arches of wooden lore,
Life's a laugh, forevermore.

The Oath of the Sentinel Oak

Upon the knoll, the oak does stand,
A sentinel with branches grand.
He swears to guard the misfit crew,
With acorn hats and shoes of dew.

Badgers wear their finest clogs,
And crack up at their own fat logs.
Birds tell jokes with twisty lies,
While grinning ants plot their sweet pies.

With whispers soft, the leaves conspire,
To tickle roots that never tire.
Laughter bounces, light and keen,
In the embrace of margined green.

The oak, with wisdom in his bark,
Shares furry tales that leave a mark.
For in this space, the spirit sings,
And joy, like breezes, brightly springs.

Conversations of Crown and Canopy

Up in the branches, birds like to chat,
Telling tall stories of where they sat.
Squirrels chip in, with their acorn stash,
While leaves giggle softly, a rustling splash.

A crow cracks a joke, the woodpecker laughs,
As shadows dance lightly on mossy paths.
The sun peeks through with a wink and a grin,
It's a comedy show where the bark's wearing thin.

The owls roll their eyes at the chatter above,
Claiming their wisdom still shines like a glove.
But crickets nearby break into a song,
In a merry old chorus, they all get along.

So next time you wander through forests so tall,
Listen for laughter, it echoes for all.
Among the green giants, fun's never far,
With chatter and chuckles, they're true superstars.

The Realm of Reverie and Root

Beneath the great trunks, where shadows play,
Moles make their meetings at the end of the day.
They gossip and giggle, with secrets to share,
While worms weave their tales, with flair and a dare.

The roots wiggle live in a dance so absurd,
Tickling the soil, they fly like a bird.
Toadstools are judges, with caps on their heads,
Nodding along as the stories are spread.

A family of foxes peeks out with delight,
Joining the revelry as day turns to night.
They leap in the moonlight, with tails held so high,
As fireflies blink like stars in the sky.

So if you should stumble on this funny spree,
Remember the whimsy of old-growth decree.
In the land of the curious, laughter's the root,
Where every creature knows their own silly flute.

Odes to Old Growth

Oh mighty old giants with spines full of tales,
Whispering secrets that glide on the gales.
Each groan and creak tells of wise old schemes,
Where critters convene for their raucous dreams.

With a twist of a branch and a flick of a leaf,
Squirrels jest loudly, their chatter a thief.
Stealing the sunlight with puns in soft twirls,
They spin tales of nuts, and the dance of the swirls.

The raccoons, so clever, offer their quips,
While beavers chime in with their toothy little grins.
They craft up a story as they gnaw on the wood,
Declaring their craft is the best in the hood.

So raise up a cheer for the legends that sway,
In the realm where the old growth comes out to play.
With laughter that echoes from trunk down to root,
Every tall tale's a song and a hoot!

Whispers from the Wildwood

In the heart of the woods where the wild things roam,
Frog bands strike up in their swampy old home.
Croaking their numbers in a beat so profound,
While crickets slap bets on who jumps the best bound.

The foxes in jackets, they shuffle and jive,
Dancing in circles, man, they're so alive!
With shadows that twist in the flickering light,
They whirl and they twirl till the dawn's taking flight.

Oh, badgers and hedgehogs all gather around,
Exchanging their recipes for nuts on the ground.
With laughter and crumbs as they munch without shame,
In the great wildwood, it's a frolicsome game.

So next time you wander through thickets and trees,
Listen for giggles dancing on the soft breeze.
For amongst the old trunks, where the chirps tend to skew,
Every rustle's a chuckle, a nature's curfew.

Stories from the Timbered Heights

In a forest so vast, where the squirrels do zoom,
A raccoon once thought he'd find a nice room.
He climbed up a branch, swayed side to side,
But fell with a thump and a nutty slide!

The owls all hooted, they laughed 'til they cried,
As he dusted his paws and tried to abide.
He grumbled aloud, 'This place has no charm!'
But was soon in a tiff, 'Cause he was back in a farm!

A woodpecker pecked on a tree made of glass,
The echo was funny, as his head made a pass.
He forgot he was drumming, with a swing and a sway,
And then ran from a squirrel who wanted to play!

So if you're out walking, in the woods take a peep,
You might see some critters who'll give you a leap.
Just smile at their antics, their pranks make it bright,
In these lofty abodes, every day is a flight!

Shadows of the Ancient Wood

In the shadows where giants of branches reside,
Lived a chubby old bear with nowhere to hide.
He slipped on a mushroom, a colorful sight,
With a roll and a tumble, he made quite a fright!

The deer giggled softly, as they peered from the fern,
This bear on his back did a feisty return.
He grumbled and chuckled, 'Oh, what a big fall!
But who says I'm clumsy? I'm graceful, after all!'

A wise old tortoise, who'd seen many days,
Stirred with a shrug, in a quirky ballet.
'Life moves slowly, but laughter's on cue,
With antics like yours, it's a show for the view!'

So when shadows grow long, and the whimsy begins,
Remember to laugh, let the fun ne'er rescind.
Beneath ancient crowns, with life all around,
The joys of the forest in silliness found!

Secrets Beneath the Boughs

Beneath leafy giants, where the critters convene,
Lived a fox with a riddle, oh so keen!
He asked all his pals, 'What's orange and loud?'
They scratched tiny heads, forming quite the crowd!

A rabbit piped up with a twitch of her ears,
'Could it be a pumpkin that's holding back cheers?'
The fox laughed so hard, with a snort and a cackle,
'No, silly dear, it's a dancing old jackal!'

A badger chimed in from a burrow so close,
'I've a secret of mine, would you like to know post?'
'It's easier to roll than to walk on a hill,
Especially when nobody's looking, what a thrill!'

So join in the laughter, beneath boughs so grand,
Where secrets are shared, and silliness spanned.
In a world full of wonders, come play with your friends,
For the joy of the forest just merrily blends!

Echoes of the Evergreen

In the realm of the green, where tall pines sway,
A porcupine danced, in the wild woods at play.
With spines sticking out, he tried to do flips,
But ended up tumbling, oh what a few trips!

The birds all squawked in their chirpy delight,
As their friend rolled around, oh what a sight!
He winked with a grin, through the laughter and cheer,
'Just practicing my circus act, watch out, I'm here!'

From shadows came whispers of giggles galore,
As the beaver announced, 'Who's up for some more?'
He built a grand dam made of sticks and of reeds,
And invited the forest for fun, yes indeed!

So when echoes arise from the woods near your home,
Listen closely for laughter where the wild critters roam.
For in pockets of green, where stories are spun,
Adventure and joy are the truest of fun!

In the Arms of Atlas Trees

Beneath leafy giants, we frolic and play,
Squirrels throw acorns, what a silly display.
Branches bend low, inviting a climb,
We swing like monkeys, defying all time.

A wise old oak shares its wobbly tale,
Of a windstorm dance that made it turn pale.
With laughter and whispers, we gather around,
Listening closely to secrets profound.

But who knew that branches could tickle so well?
As we laugh and shout, we stumble and fell.
The grass is like velvet, we roll in delight,
Beneath the grand canopy, everything's right.

When shadows grow long and the sun starts to fade,
We become treetop shadows, a whimsical parade.
In the arms of the forest, we're free and we're bold,
The heart of the trees holds adventures untold.

The Eternal Gaze of the Grove

In a thicket of fables, the laughter erupts,
With squirrels acting like pompous little pups.
Dancing in circles, they trip on their tails,
As giggles echo through fantastical trails.

The wise willows sway with a comical flair,
Preening their leaves like it's all a great dare.
Each gust of the breeze brings a wobbly jig,
Who knew that trees could bust moves, oh so big?

Among shady giants, we spot a surprise,
A tortoise on stilts, it's all in our eyes.
With a slow-motion dash toward a sunset so grand,
We cheer for the tortoise, it's a sight previously planned!

The sun dips low, painting laughter in gold,
In the embrace of the grove, we never grow old.
The trees keep on chuckling, it's sheer comedy,
In their eternal gaze, we find our melody.

The Network of Forgotten Roots

Beneath the deep ground, where the roots intertwine,
The gossip of soil is truly divine.
Old tales of critters that once walked this lane,
Spread whispers of wisdom, both joyful and plain.

The rabbits hold meetings, discussing their plots,
While moles dig the dirt with prescient thoughts.
A turtle chimes in, what a strange little crew,
Plotting their antics, and tea for a few.

In this network below, laughter bubbles up,
As secrets of flora brew in a cup.
A cactus speaks softly, 'You won't believe lies,
The flowers just told me that cows wear big ties.'

At last, with a giggle, they all stampede free,
Emerging from shadows, what a sight to see!
With roots all ablaze in jokes and delight,
They dance in the meadow, till dark swallows light.

Sidelong Glances at the Sky

Under the tall pines, we lay in a row,
With clouds as our kings, putting on quite a show.
They morph into creatures, a feast for the eyes,
A dragon? A pancake? Oh, what a surprise!

As we chuckle and point, a squirrel drops by,
With sidelong glances, he peers at the sky.
"Are we just figments of leafy daydreams,
Or guardians of laughter, among sunlight's beams?"

The branches above are our fickle emcees,
Hosting a comedy, light as the breeze.
Every laugh resonates, from bark to the root,
Nature's own stand-up, with giggles to boot.

At dusk when we leave, the trees wave goodbye,
With whispers and rustles, like a hoot from on high.
In the embrace of the forest, we find our cheer,
With sidelong glances, we'll soon reappear!

The Green Cathedral

In the forest choir, squirrels sing,
Bouncing on branches, like springs of a swing.
Owls wear glasses, wise and grand,
While raccoons throw parties, oh, isn't it grand?

Pine cones drop like clumsy gifts,
As chipmunks share their acorn lifts.
Sunbeams dance on the leafy floor,
Squirrels giggle, asking for more.

A woodpecker pecks with style and flair,
Telling knock-knock jokes that float in the air.
The trees sway gently, laughing out loud,
While the parrot performs for an imaginary crowd.

So join the fun in nature's spree,
Where every creature sings with glee.
The green cathedral is a humorous sight,
With laughter and joy in the soft sunlight.

In the Shade of Giants

Beneath the giants, a picnic ensues,
With ants in tuxedos, sharing their views.
A deer wears a hat, quite fashionable too,
While rabbits play cards, 'til they all turn blue.

The wind whispers secrets, a giggling breeze,
Jokes shared with the mushrooms, swaying with ease.
A butterfly lands, twirling like a dancer,
While a hedgehog comments, "What a romancer!"

Under canopies deep, the laughter bubbles,
As the fox tells tales that cause silly troubles.
The shadows grow long, the light starts to fade,
Yet the laughter continues, in this leafy glade.

So come take a rest, in the shade so divine,
Join the joyful mammals, sip nature's wine.
In the laughter of giants, forever we'll stay,
For in this comical forest, we're never astray!

The Echoes of Branch and Leaf

In the bustling woods where the branches bend,
There's a chorus of chirps that never will end.
A frog plays the drums on the old fallen log,
While a shy little snail croons like a fog.

The branches shake with stories untold,
While bamboo flutes hum, both silly and bold.
A raccoon juggles acorns with a sly grin,
As the wise old owl chuckles, "Let's begin!"

Leaves whisper secrets to the curious breeze,
While the porcupines dance, some silly, some ease.
The ripples of laughter float high in the air,
As a badger recites rhymes with flair.

So follow the echoes, let humor unfurl,
Among twisted trunks, where joy begins to swirl.
In the heart of the forest, where the fun never leaves,
Hear the echoes of laughter, through branches and leaves!

Murmurs from the Mossy Floor

Down on the forest floor, where the moss grows thick,
Fungi giggle and dance, they've got quite the trick.
A lizard wears glasses, trying to read,
As the bumblebees plan their next honey deed.

Tiny mushrooms whisper, sharing their dreams,
Of hopping on clouds made of fluff and of creams.
The snails try parkour, but slide down with grace,
While gophers hold races, at a comical pace.

The earthworms debate on who is the best,
With a tiny owl referee, full of jest.
The ladybugs judge with hearts all aglow,
While the frogs are the crowd, shouting "Bravo!"

So come to the floor, where the laughter runs free,
Join the fun of the critters, in the great leafy spree.
In the murmur of moss, let your worries adrift,
For here in the wild, we share nature's gift!

www.ingramcontent.com/pod-product-compliance
Lightning Source LLC
Chambersburg PA
CBHW071825160426
43209CB00003B/207